EDGAR CAYCE'S
HOMETOWN

HOPKINSVILLE
KENTUCKY

by

William T. Turner

and

Chris Gilkey

13-digit International Standard Book Number   978-1-934898-08-6
Library of Congress Card Catalog Number   2010926474

Cover design and book layout by James Asher

Manufactured in the United States of America

All book order correspondence should be addressed to:

McClanahan Publishing House, Inc.
P.O. Box 100
Kuttawa, KY 42055

800-544-6959

www.kybooks.com

Dedication

Lena Jones Wicks
1895-1985

The passage of life portrays a chain of personalities who convey their passion for purpose. Lena Jones Wicks, to whom this work is dedicated, motivated William T. Turner, who in turn instilled that love for local history in Chris Gilkey.

William T. Turner

Chris Gilkey

Acknowledgments

We would like to express gratitude to the following people for their support, interest, and motivation to share information in the compilation of this work: Marion Adams, Eloise Bowles, William R. Bowles, Ann Smithson Campbell, Ernest C. Cansler, Nannie Stowe Caudle, Charles Thomas Cayce, D.D. Cayce, III, Edgar Cayce Foundation, Edgar Evans Cayce, Elizabeth Gary Cayce, Florence Cayce, Hugh Lynn Cayce, Robert Clinton Cayce, Jean Swift Chism, David Clark, Sara Cooper, Elizabeth Garnett Countzler, Mary Alice Major Duncan, Ella Foster, Florence Elgin Garrott, Miriam Cayce Gregory, Soula Kay Johnston Hazelip, Alice Freeman Hills, Peggy Caudle Hyams, Ruth Johnson Jones, Mary Joiner Jones, John W. Johnson, Kentucky New Era, Alton Ketchum, W.E. Knox, Arthur B. Lander, Jr., James L. Major, Jennie Major, Lillian Major, W. Gladstone Major, U.L. Major, William S. McCarroll, William B. Moore, Melissa Moss Moseley, Evelyn Lacy Noland, Jack Orem, Emily B. Perry, Planters Bank & Trust Co., Dorothy Cayce Sherman, Frances Farmer Segler, Alice Cayce Smithson, Leonora Wall Starnes, Annie Pierce Steger, Katherine Major Swift, Jeanette Thomas, Sara Dalton Todd, J. Minos Turner, Lena Jones Wicks, Capt. Mac W. Wood, Ben S. Wood, III, and Lucile Thomas Young.

Table of Contents

Introduction

Christian County and its county seat, Hopkinsville, are located in southwestern Kentucky, a part of the Pennyroyal region. The county is bounded on the north by Hopkins and Muhlenberg Counties, on the east by Todd County, on the west by Trigg County, and on the south by Montgomery and Stewart Counties, Tennessee. This county, the second largest in the state of Kentucky, was carved from Logan County by the Kentucky General Assembly in 1796 with actual organization on March 1, 1797. The new county was named in memory of Colonel William Christian, a veteran of the American Revolution and a brother-in-law of Patrick Henry, Governor of Virginia. Originally, the county included all land north of the Tennessee line, west of Logan County and the Green River, south of the Ohio River, and east of the Tennessee River. All of the present counties in this area were formed out of Christian County between 1798 and1860.

Christian County made a remarkably rapid recovery after the Civil War. The reasons for this recovery are reflected through the stable labor market, the innovative approaches of farmers, and the survival of pre-war wealth invested in the construction of turnpikes, railroads, schools, houses, tobacco warehouses, later called loose floors, and flour mills. No major military engagements occurred in the county.

Agriculture and farm related business, along with the rural social advances, moved country people from isolation to full participation in community life. County farmers promoted the Grange movement during the 1870s, and the annual county fair drew large participation from country and town people. The first local dark tobacco market sale in 1870, coupled with large, low-paid labor force, brought success to tobacco production. The eventual price collapse of that market throughout the "Black Patch" brought about the Night Rider War between 1906 and 1911.

Turnpike construction progressed actively during the 1870s with the freeing of these toll roads accomplished in 1901. Rural Free Delivery of mail arrived the same year.

Railroad construction and operation in the late 1860s opened markets for agricultural and industrial products in addition to providing convenient transportation. Railroad service was inaugurated in Hopkinsville with the arrival of the first train from Guthrie on April 8, 1868. Constructed by the Evansville, Henderson, and Nashville Railroad, this line was later extended north to Henderson and was acquired by the Louisville and Nashville Railroad in 1879. Another L&N route, "Buckberry's Special," was completed across South Christian County, connecting Clarksville and Princeton in 1886. This line was abandoned in 1933 and was replaced by Highway 117. The Ohio Valley Railroad was built from Gracey to Hopkinsville in 1892 and purchased by the Illinois Central Railroad in 1897. In 1903, the western division of the Tennessee Central Railway entered Christian County at Edgoten (Edge-of-Tennessee) connecting Clarksville and Hopkinsville. Many small county towns owe their creation and prosperity to the railroads. These late 19th century communities include: Pembroke, Casky, Kelly, Crofton, Empire, and Mannington on the Henderson Division of the L&N: Kennedy, Oak Grove, Bell Station, Howell, Herndon, Rich, Newstead, Julien, and Gracey on the C&P Branch, also on the L&N; Green's Crossing on the Illinois Central; and Edgoten, Thompkinsville, Naomi, Masonville, and Fidelio on the Tennessee Central.

The African American community experienced development through the organization of a school system in 1872 and many new churches were constituted. In 1885, the first African American served on a grand jury, and by 1898 the race had been represented in the political offices of coroner, jailer, constable, and pensioner.

The city of Hopkinsville progressed through many social and civic improvements during the post-war period. A public library was established in 1874, two years after the city school system was organized. A Commercial Club, followed by a Board of Trade and the Hopkinsville Business Men's Association dates from 1888.

A shift in political influence came in the post-war period. Christian County was a Republican stronghold both on national and local elections from 1865 through the 1928 election.

Utility service installation included a telephone exchange in 1887, electricity in 1892, a water system in 1896, and city sewerage service in 1906. Leisure and recreational activities included the "Hoptown Hoppers" baseball team in the Kitty League, 1903-1954, picnics at Pilot Rock, activities at the YMCA, country jaunts by the bicycle club, and vacations at Cerulean Springs in Trigg County and Dawson Springs in Hopkins County.

The first thirty-five years in the life of Edgar Cayce were spent in Kentucky. Nearly seventeen passed in his native Christian County, ten in Louisville and Bowling Green, and over eight in Hopkinsville, the county seat of Christian. It was there in the formative years of his life that this native son developed his remarkable psychic talents and embarked upon a lifetime of service to God and to mankind. This talented man returned to his homeland for many visits, but the years 1877 to 1912 marked the foundation for his courage and strength.

Across this span of thirty-five years, this agricultural community, with its economy based on corn, wheat, dark tobacco, livestock, and hog production, registered a census gain of 4,000 to total 38,000 people. Hopkinsville, a quiet town with its farm related stores and shops nearly doubled its population to slightly fewer than 10,000 residents during the years of Edgar Cayce's residency there.

In young manhood, Edgar Cayce experienced a seemingly incurable loss of voice. Through self diagnosis while under hypnosis, he prescribed simple treatment which ultimately restored his voice. From the first psychic reading given in Hopkinsville on March 31, 1901 until the last in Roanoke, Virginia, September 17, 1944, Edgar Cayce gave 14,256 medical and life readings.

CHAPTER

1

A WAY OF LIFE FOR THE CAYCE'S

CENTER OF FARM OPERATION. The farm stable served a multiple role. It housed cattle, hogs, horses, mules, sheep, and goats for protection against winter weather. The hayloft on the second floor, with the projecting bonnet used for hoisting hay for storage, was also a favorite play area for children in rainy weather. Two rooms on the ground level, opposite one another across the hallway, one served as a gear room and storage area for harness and the other used as a corn crib. This farm landmark, familiar to Edgar Cayce as a child, is rapidly disappearing from the farm landscape.

A GOOD KENTUCKY FOUR-MULE TEAM. The year was 1911. The location was near LaFayette, Kentucky about 10 miles southwest of Edgar Cayce's birthplace. A four-mule team had just returned from a field where yellow corn was picked by hand. This crop was principally used for livestock feed. The Mogul wagon, manufactured by J.K. and M.C. Forbes in Hopkinsville, contained a six barrel load which required a half day to hand pick.

MAKING BACON. The principle food source for farm families in Edgar's boyhood was hog meat along with garden vegetables and fruit from orchards. Hog killing, a farm operation that included all hands, usually occurred in November and December. Temperature for meat preservation was best between 25 and 32 degrees. If colder, the meat would freeze and if warmer, the meat would spoil. Hog meat was covered with salt in large wooden boxes in a smokehouse for the curing process.

PIONEER INDUSTRY. An unidentified group of people are caught standing at attention before the camera lens to record a day in the life of country people a century and a quarter ago. The saw mill, with blades shown at right, was powered by a wood-fired steam engine. The front right wheel had been removed to provide clearance for the belt on the fly wheel of the engine to the saw. The saw mill was an essential part of the construction business throughout neighborhood farms. Logs were sawed for farm building and home construction.

THIRTEEN MONTH CROP. Edgar Cayce's childhood era on the farm saw the production of the number one money crop, dark tobacco. This scene featured a plant bed, usually prepared in January, where tobacco seed was sewn and covered by canvas in March until near setting time in early June. The crop, from plant bed preparation to sale at the loose floor, often required thirteen months.

THE BLACK PATCH. This scene of a dark tobacco patch is featured from circa 1895 in the Bell Station community on the site of the present Ft. Campbell airport. The stage of development was called "spreading the hill". Crops required constant attention from setting, chopping or hoeing, suckering, topping, worming, and dusting to cutting and spiking in preparation for hanging in the barn to cure

SMOKE. Dark tobacco was spiked on sticks and handed up five or six tiers and suspended on tier poles or rails after cutting in early August. In fall cool weather, low fires were laid in a pit on the barn floor with the use of saw dust and tree slabs or laps for fuel to create vast amounts of smoke. During the smoking process, a man stayed in the barn to watch and to maintain the fire. If a tobacco stick broke and fell into the fire, without immediate attention, the entire barn and year's worth of hard work burned to the ground within 45 minutes. Edgar as a child experienced burning eyes and choked breathing from maintaining his watch in the barn.

THE TOBACCO FACTORY. Once Edgar and other family members completed the task of stripping the tobacco, removing leaves from the stems, and grading it into tips, lugs, and seconds, the dark tobacco was loaded onto two and four mule team wagons. It was then hauled to market in Hopkinsville. Wagon loads of quilt-covered tobacco are featured in this scene at the J.D. Ware & Company-Tobacco Broker Warehouse on Tenth Street between the L&N Railroad and Campbell Street. The foreground shows Peace Park in early stages of development. This warehouse, pictured in 1909, was one of a dozen in town when Edgar was a boy. The old landmark was torn down October 27, 1977.

PRIZING DARK TOBACCO. The W.T. Cooper & Company Warehouse shows hand-tied tobacco, packed or prized, in large wooden barrels called hogsheads. Hogsheads in Western Kentucky were referred to as "hogszids". The tobacco was then loaded into railroad boxcars and shipped to producers of cigars, cigarettes, pipe tobacco, and snuff for "dipping", principally by women.

AMERICA'S BREAD BASKET. Winter wheat, usually sewn in October and harvested in June, was the secondary money crop following dark tobacco. It was also raised for home consumption, principally rolls, biscuits, and light bread. Originally, a man could cut, using a sythe, a curved handle blade, two acres in a day. In Edgar's era, Cyrus McCormick's reaper or binder, pulled by a four-mule team and cutting an eight foot swath, could harvest ten to twelve acres in a day. That invention, in the wheat fields of Christian County, provided America's bread basket.

SHOCKED. As the wheat was cut by the binder, the straw was tied together in bundles and dropped from the platform to the ground. A follow-up crew gathered these bundles, stood them upright and placed about 12 to 15 bundles in a pile called a shock. Two to three bundles were positioned on top to shed the rain. The shock remained in the field from cutting time until late July when the bundles were hauled to the separator for threshing. Edgar's folks called it threshing.

WHEAT THRESHING RIG. The summer's big event occurred when two dozen men and boys descended upon a field of shocked wheat. The rig consisted of the separator, which separated the grain from the straw; the steam engine, belted to the separator for power; coal and water wagons, to feed the hungry and thirsty engine; and mule drawn wagons, which brought the bundles of wheat to the separator. Edgar's childhood wheat threshing days were spent as a water boy for the thirsty workers.

COME AND GET IT. The hungry-filled laborers worked in eager anticipation of the sounding of the steam engine whistle declaring that dinner time had arrived. Large threshing operations maintained a cook shack where a man, laboring over a step stove, prepared pans of fried chicken, green beans, potatoes, white beans, hot biscuits, and buttermilk. No doubt, Edgar was on hand for this occasion.

AIN'T IT GOOD. A highlight and a great treat of country living in Christian County was, over a century ago, the consumption of watermelon, rarely cold, on a hot summer day. This scene could have easily been Edgar and his mother on a watermelon pile as together they enjoyed slurping it without the use of a fork or spoon just as the two people featured. There were other great country summertime treats of that era, homemade ice cream, barbecues, going fishing and swimming, and attending the county fair.

CHURCH HILL GRANGE. The Patrons of Husbandry, commonly known as the Grange, became popular throughout Christian County in the 1870s. The illustrated Church Hill Grange was organized in 1873 and disbanded in 1926. This farm organization, of which several Cayce men were members, constructed a meeting hall in 1878. Grangers promoted rural social interaction and served as a pressure force for the increase of farm produce prices. The landmark was destroyed by fire on March 4, 1987.

CHAPTER

2

THE WORLD OF BUSINESS
IN EDGAR'S ERA

HOTEL LATHAM. Built by the Hopkinsville Hotel Company in 1894, this yellow-brick, Italian-Renaissance landmark, with a red tile roof, was located on the eastside of Virginia Street between Sixth and Seventh Streets. Albert Davis Noe, Sr., owner and manager of Hotel Latham from 1912 until his death in 1932, was a business partner with Edgar Cayce and Dr. Wesley Ketchum in the Psychic Reading Corporation, 1910-1912. Noe and Ketchum financially supported Edgar in a state of the art photographic studio in return for a division of the profits derived from psychic readings.

LATHAM LOBBY. This lobby was the gathering place for many visitors who came to Hopkinsville between 1901 and 1912 to explore the gift of Edgar Cayce. The hotel and its lobby represented Hopkinsville and were frequented by Edgar Cayce for meals and was the site of many psychic readings. The 93 room hotel, built at a cost of $104,000, was destroyed by fire on August 4, 1940.

BANK OF HOP. Hopkinsville, in the era of Edgar Cayce, supported four banks. The oldest, the Bank of Hopkinsville, was chartered in 1865 and operated until its purchase by the City Bank & Trust Company in 1930. The Bank of Hopkinsville was located on the southeast corner of South Main and Seventh Streets. It is doubtful that Edgar experienced much customer connection with any of the banks as his financial stability was always challenged.

BUSINESS FRONT APPEAL. The span of time, covered by Edgar living in Hopkinsville, saw the development of a more elaborate style of store fronts and business houses. This scene of the Bank of Hopkinsville, circa 1890, portrays the use of metal and wood in store front architecture. Note the reflection of business houses across the street in the windows of the bank.

THE FARMER'S BANK. A landmark familiar to Edgar Cayce was the Planters Bank & Trust Company, located on the northeast corner of South Main at Eighth Street. The structure stood on this corner from 1902 until 1956. Attorney offices, located upstairs, were apart of Edgar's life during his adult years here. Note the second floor level clock which informed several generations by tolling the Westminster chime, "Lord through this hour, be though our guide, so by thy power, no foot shall slide."

PLANTER'S INTERIOR – 1904. Edgar Cayce knew these men, from left to right, Dennis Shaw, Frank Trice, Ira L. Smith, a customer, Joseph F. Garnett, President, and John B. Trice, Vice-President. Note the clock, the large calendar, the wicker waste basket, and the combination gas jet electric lights. The large ledger with handwritten entries on the desk, at right, was the system of record keeping before the world of computers.

CITY-BANK & TRUST COMPANY. Hopkinsville's third financial institution, City-Bank, was organized in 1880. It was located on the northeast corner of South Main and East Seventh Streets until 1930. The one-bay building featured was the face of this bank from 1909 until 1919. It was then remodeled to include two bays and remains today. Customary of the time, Edgar and his wife frequently passed this building on evening strolls in downtown Hopkinsville.

CITY-BANK INTERIOR. The interior style of banks during Edgar's young manhood portrayed an elaborate mixture of tile floors, marble teller cages, and pressed metal ceilings. Note the brass cuspidor on the floor doubtfully ever used by Edgar Cayce.

FIRST NATIONAL BANK. The southwest corner of South Main and West Ninth Street was the home of the only federally chartered bank in Christian County. In 1888, when Edgar Cayce was eleven years old, business leaders organized the First National Bank. Merger with the City-Bank saw the establishment of the First-City Bank & Trust Company in 1930.

ANOTHER ERA. Businessmen of 1890 appear at First National Bank in their formal grooming as they pause in business transactions to record their presence for future generations. It is doubtful that the men in Edgar Cayce's family dressed in this dignified manner very frequently. This location is now occupied by Southern Exposure photographic studio.

HOT, DIRTY, GREASY. Forbes Blacksmith Shop, shown in this scene on South Virginia Street at Tenth, includes among others Mack Page, John Mitchell, Sam Hadden, and Dabney Cary, men known to Edgar Cayce. The farm related shop workers maintained a six-day work week without paid vacation and retirement benefits.

FARMER'S HANGOUT. Forbes Planing Mill and Blacksmith Shop, on the present site of Hilliard Lyons located on South Virginia and Tenth Streets, was for several generations the gathering place for farmers who came to town to transact their farm related business. Forbes was noted for its home-manufactured Mogul wagon. Edgar Cayce's family owned Mogul wagons and was influenced by the company slogans; "Strong Where the Strain Comes" and "Buy a Mogul and Will It to Your Grandson".

MEDICAL DISCOVERY. This picture from 1894 features African-American laborers at the brick kilns of Dalton Brick Company, located on North Elm Street. The laborers became ill showing signs of great weakness. Doctors were unable to determine the cause. Edgar Cayce's psychic readings for these men identified the underlying cause of the illness as Pellagra. Further readings prescribed a greater amount of fresh fruit and vegetables in their diet by which the men were cured.

PAVING THE WAY. The 1890s brought the popularity of the great bicycle era. Several bicycle shops were opened, a bicycle riding club was established, and weekend jaunts to Pilot Rock, the Canton Ferry, and Clarksville, Tennessee, became a part of young people's culture. Edgar Cayce owned a bicycle and frequently rode it out to the edge of town to have a date. E. Munsey Moss, at right, grandfather of Hopkinsville pianist, Marshall Butler, stands with his employee, Jim Simmons, at left, and a customer in Moss' Bicycle Shop on East Sixth Street circa 1895.

BICYCLE REPAIR SHOP. A Hopkinsville bicycle repair shop illustrates bicycles and the many parts needed for successful riding. It appeared a new supply of bikes has just arrived along with many parts including horns, lights, intertube repair kits, and rims and tires. A new invention of the 1880s, the telephone, hangs on the wall at right.

THE FAMOUS HILL HOUSE. A center for male social life in Hopkinsville at the turn of the Twentieth Century was the lobby of the Hill House, located at the northeast corner of East Ninth and North Liberty Streets. Edgar Cayce made this photograph printed from a glass negative. His quality of photography, exhibiting time, talent and patience, took special ability. The Hill House, a boarding and rooming house operated by Mrs. Helen Hill, was in business from 1898 until 1916. The popular eatery had great appeal for traveling people and drummers, early salesmen.

EARLY RESTAURANT. Edgar Cayce photographed this unidentified restaurant in Hopkinsville circa 1900. Deterioration was created by emulsion separation on the glass plate negative. Boys behind the counter appear to be helping their dad in the serving of Baltimore raw oysters while a photograph of Theodore Roosevelt takes stock of the scene.

LEADING MERCHANT. Hopkinsville photographer, Clarence Anderson shot this image of Charles M. Latham's Dry Goods Store in the early 1890s. The Latham block, consisting of four store rooms, still stands on the west side of South Main at West Seventh Street. This image reveals a Hopkinsville storefront about the time Edgar Cayce moved to Hopkinsville. Latham was the first local merchant to provide his employees a one-week paid vacation.

M. FRANKEL'S & SONS DRY GOODS AND NOTIONS. Malcolm Frankel and his family operated a dry goods and notions – sewing materials, store on the northwest corner of South Main and West Eighth Streets. In business from circa 1880 until 1920, this firm was the leading clothing store in Hopkinsville in the years Edgar Cayce lived here.

FRANKEL'S BUSY STORE. "The Busy Store" was a later slogan applied to Frankel's business. In 1908, the pictured gentlemen appeared for a photograph in the Men's Department of Frankel's Busy Store. They included, from left to right, Tom Roberts, J.D. McGowen, Roy J. Cary, and Charlie Slaughter.

MAMMOTH CLOTHING CO. J.T. Wall & Company was a strong competitor of Frankel's Dry Goods in the 1890s. It operated on the southwest corner of South Main and West Seventh Streets during the years Edgar Cayce was a clerk in the book and stationery store of Hopper Brothers, directly across the street.

C.K. WYLY DRUG STORE. One of Hopkinsville's more popular drug stores, Wyly's, was located on Main Street between Seventh and Court Streets when this image was shot in 1901. Located in the next block from where Edgar Cayce clerked at Hopper's Book Store, he frequently stopped in for a soda, cigarettes, or maybe a box of candy for Gertrude. While there, he entered into the circle of acquaintances as together they shared the street talk of the day.

A PAUSE TO WET YOUR WHISTLE. In this 1901 scene of Wyly's Drug Store, customers have gathered to sip a soda through a straw. The elaborate fixtures, the drink dispenser, and the candy jars on the counter top were typical of drug store furnishings of that era. A well known character to Edgar Cayce was the customer enjoying a drink at right, Will A. Wilgus, former Postmaster and a tour guide director, is remembered as the benefactor of the Wilgus playgrounds. They were located on West Seventh Street, West Eighteenth Street, and South Campbell Street in Hopkinsville.

ANDERSON-FOWLER DRUG STORE. For over sixty years, the southeast corner of Ninth and Main Streets was the site of a popular drug store. The prescriptions called for in Edgar Cayce's psychic readings were often filled here. Though Higgins Drug Store was located here after 1920, the previous drug stores, well-known to Cayce, were Anderson-Fowler and later Campbell-Coates.

DRUG STORE DÉCOR. This 1920 photograph features the Ninth and Main Streets business of Higgins Drug Store. Its interior decoration, featuring a fleur de li tile design in the floor, marble based glass display counters, a newspaper rack, a heat radiator at left, a cuspidor used for tobacco spit, and pressed metal ceiling, revealed the décor of popular taste a century ago. Druggist E.H. Higgins was a third cousin of Edgar.

COFFEE, CANNED GOODS, AND CATELOPES. Edgar Cayce, as young photographer in Hopkinsville at the turn of the Twentieth Century, was motivated to photograph the interior of several Hopkinsville stores. The photo image applied to a glass plate negative created a clear picture but left no place for identification. Thus, this unidentified Hopkinsville grocery store portrayed a view of social history.

HARDWARE GIANT. The hardware business in Hopkinsville was dominated by Forbes & Bro. for 75 years. Organized by brothers James K. and Madison C. Forbes in 1871, the firm grew to lead the business and industrial community. Hardware sale, the principle line of business, operated at the location featured on the southeast corner of South Main and Tenth Streets. Forbes & Bro. sold merchandise from 22 different business locations ranging from buggies, plows, Mogul farm wagons, cooking stoves, jewelry, automobiles, and water buckets. The firm manufactured church furniture in Hopkinsville and Owensboro. Edgar Cayce and his family were frequent customers of the Forbes brother's outlets.

THE RED FRONT. (left and below) For generations, originating in the time when Edgar Cayce lived in Hopkinsville, the Red Front Grocery Store was a landmark on Main Street between Sixth and Seventh Streets. Built in 1892 and long operated by William T. Cooper, the structure was painted red, thus the name. The 1900 exterior image showed staple grocery items on the brick sidewalk, while professional offices were located on the second floor. The Pythian Lodge, a fraternal order, was situated on the third floor. The sidewalk featured a very unusual ground level skylight, made up of small squares of tinted glass, allowing light into the basement. The interior, dating from the same era, provided a interesting display of canned goods in pyramid fashion.

THE RACKET STORE. In 1895, a New York City retail franchise, The Racket Store, opened in a new three-story brick storehouse on the northeast corner of South Main and Tenth Streets. J.H. Kugler came from New York to manage this operation. The firm bore this name because of the wide variety of merchandise sold. Kugler and Edgar Cayce became friends and fishing partners. Curved glass show windows were a new retail architectural feature brought to Hopkinsville in the 1890s.

F.A. YOST COMPANY. Delbert D. Cayce, an uncle of Edgar, joined F.A. Yost in the operation of this hardware store in 1907. Ten years later, it became Cayce-Yost Company and three generations followed until the store closed in 1994. It was located on the northeast corner of South Main and Tenth Streets, 1907-1950, which houses the popular restaurant today, Harper House.

STOVES AND SURREYS. F.A. Yost Company, later Cayce-Yost Company, advertised and sold three floors of hardware and related merchandise. Surreys, with the fringe on top, coal-fired stoves, along with Sherwin-Williams paint, are featured in this scene circa 1907. Edgar Cayce and his family were frequent visitors and customers in this family connected business.

PLANTERS HARDWARE COMPANY. The agricultural community of Hopkinsville, in the first decade of the Twentieth Century, depended heavily on the retail hardware business to fulfill their needs on everything from cooking stoves to farm implements. One of the leading firms, Planters Hardware was located in the Ragsdale-Cooper building on the southwest corner of South Main and Tenth Streets. Established in 1903, and in operation at this location until destroyed by fire on November 6, 1927, Planters provided many products needed for the Cayce family.

HERE COMES THE ICE WAGON. A familiar sight on the streets of Hopkinsville, through the years when Edgar Cayce's family lived here, was the horse-drawn delivery wagon of the Ellis Ice & Coal Company. The plant, located on the L&N Railroad, between Eleventh and Twelfth Streets, provided ice for refrigerators and making homemade ice cream in the summertime and coal for heating in the wintertime.

E.C. GRAY LIVERY STABLE. Livery stables in Hopkinsville, a century ago, were the forerunner of service stations and car dealerships today. Hand-painted signs identified the location of these establishments. Gray's was located on East Ninth Street, west of the L&N Passenger Depot, on the site of the old Coca-Cola plant. It was from this stable that a horse and buggy were "borrowed" by the Night Riders in the early morning hours of December 7, 1907. This action was needed to remove the wounded, alleged leader of the Night Riders, Dr. David A. Amoss, after he had been accidentally shot by one of his own men on the railroad station platform. The house and buggy were graciously returned the next day after use and left standing in Little River behind the old County Jail.

SNEAD AND KELLEY LIVERY STABLE. Hopkinsville sign painter, Henry Grubbs painted the unique signage on the wall of this stable, located on Main Street, between Fourth and Fifth Streets. The livery stable provided horses for rent for salesmen, pleasure riding, and for auction. On occasion, Edgar Cayce would hire a horse and buggy from John H. Snead and John R. Kelley for a ride with his date along a moon-lit country road, or later for a family ride.

RICHARD LEAVELL'S LIVERY STABLE. The best known and longest operating livery stable in Hopkinsville was located on Ninth Street, east of the fire station. "Dick" Leavell, as he was known, was considered the authority on horses and mules. From this location, he conducted a large rental service, horse and mule sales, and auctions. Dr. G.P. Isbell, veterinary surgeon, was located at this business. The structure was gutted by fire on August 28, 1926 and again on August 11, 1945.

HATS! HATS! HATS! Edgar Cayce's sister, Annie, owned and operated a millinery store in the Pennyroyal Apartment building, located on the southwest corner of South Main and Eleventh Streets from circa 1918 until it burned in November, 1927. For many years, prior to operating her own business, "Miss Annie", as she was known, was manager of the hat department of J.H. Anderson & Company department store. She later sold hats at Loveman's Department Store in Nashville, Tennessee.

MUSICALLY INCLINED. Edgar Cayce photographed a number of Hopkinsville businesses in the early 1900s. He was good at expressing an interest in the culture of his time but failed to identify the location. A Hopkinsville music store, in this image, featured hand and player pianos, along with parlor foot pump organs. The gas light fixtures of the era revealed the method of interior lighting prior to the coming of electricity.

HOPKINSVILLE KENTUCKIAN. Edgar Cayce's Hopkinsville, 1877-1912, included a dozen newspapers, all of which held a special interest to him. The *Hopkinsville Kentuckian* was published from 1879 until 1919 by Charles M. Meacham, mayor and historian. The paper, weekly and later bi-weekly, was published in a building on South Main Street between Ninth and Tenth Streets, next door to the present Harper House. This building was for many years the site of the Tom C. Jones Insurance Agency, a first cousin of Edgar.

KENTUCKY NEW ERA. The longest running newspaper in Hopkinsville dates from 1869. During the young adult life of Edgar Cayce, the *Kentucky New Era* was published in the building on the southeast corner of West Seventh and Bethel Streets, constructed in 1910.

HOP. T. LEE'S SALOON. This West Seventh Street saloon and mail order house was in business circa 1910. It was owned by B.M. Lee of Bloomington Springs, Tennessee and G.W. Harper of Nashville, Tennessee. One of eighteen saloons in Hopkinsville in the era of Edgar's last residency here, this mail order business originated when the Tennessee legislature banned the sale of Tennessee liquor within that state. Thus, it was shipped to Kentucky and sold through this very successful operation.

CANNON BROS. SALOON. James W. Cannon and J. Thomas Cannon operated this saloon, located on East Seventh Street between Main and Virginia Streets, in 1909. Purveyors of fine spirits were open a twelve hour day six days a week. Though not apart of Edgar Cayce's lifestyle, local saloons were a great part of local culture before national prohibition.

STAG SALOON. (above and below) One hundred and ten years ago, Hopkinsville photographer, Edgar Cayce captured the images of several local businesses. They were processed on 4x6 glass plate negatives and stored in his photographic studio. Years later after the room had long been vacant, they were found by Captain Mac W. Wood and given to the co-author, William T. Turner. The first of the two featured prints, from one of these negatives, was the Stag Saloon. By 1910, when the second photograph was made, the Stag Saloon, was still located on South Main Street in the Holland's Opera House building. By this time, a new bar and back bar had been installed. The bartenders featured in this image were Edward H. Williams, at left, and Clem Davis, at right.

TOBIN'S TAILOR SHOP. Edgar Cayce's photographic talent contributed this turn of the century view of a tailor shop featuring Jack Tobin, owner, at left. Men of that era took great pride in being measured for and having made a tailor-made suit. This business was for many years located on Main Street between Sixth and Seventh Streets. Tobin's business signature survives in an ornate glass sign above the law office of Ben Guier.

HOPKINSVILLE PLOW FACTORY. Hopkinsville's entry into the Industrial Age occurred in 1874 when a group of business men organized and built a plow manufacturing factory. The firm survived about four years and the structure was maintained as a tobacco factory. Later, it was used as Higgins' Wholesale Beer Warehouse. The building was torn down on October 22, 1977.

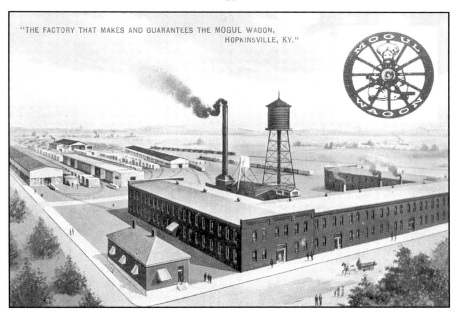

MOGUL WAGON FACTORY. Brothers, J.K. and M.C. Forbes organized Hopkinsville's largest industrial complex in 1871. Wagon production was located on the southwest corner of South Virginia and Tenth Streets, now the Hilliard-Lyons building, until 1906. The featured factory was built on northeast corner of 21st and Harrison Streets that year and was in operation until it was destroyed by fire on December 28, 1925.

MOGUL WAGON. This catalog advertisement featured an illustration of one of the styles of Mogul wagons. The firm manufactured log, mountain, platform spring, farm, and dead axle coal and ice wagons, drays, floats, and gun carriages. Edgar Cayce's uncles bought and used Mogul farm wagons for many years.

CHAPTER

3

EDGAR'S EYE
OF NINTH AND MAIN STREETS

THE BIG SNOW. Edgar Cayce was almost nine years old when the deepest snow recorded in
the 19th Century fell upon Christian County. On February 2, 1886, a twenty-one inch snow
was recorded by local weather observers. This scene showed Main Street, looking north to Seventh Street, with the courthouse porch columns and cupola revealed at right.

DOWNTOWN HOPKINSVILLE. When Edgar, as a child, made a trip to town, he was intrigued by the large brick buildings, multi-colored awnings, and stepping stones across the streets. This view, on August 7, 1886, featured the downtown section, looking south on Main Street from Seventh Street.

CENTER OF THE UNIVERSE. Main Street, looking north across Ninth Street, presented an image of Hopkinsville's main intersection to Edgar when he came to town as a nine year old boy. Banks, dry goods stores, the Phoenix Hotel, and Holland's Opera House were well-known landmarks along this picturesque view. Note the absence of livestock confining laws, automobiles, street lights, and paved thoroughfares.

A FAMILIAR VIEW. Around 1900, a photographer stepped into the middle of Main Street and pointed his camera lens south toward Seventh Street. By the click of the shutter, this view of Edgar Cayce's hometown was frozen in time. His photographic studio was later located in the Thompson building on the left side of this picture just beyond the intersection.

ABOUT TO LEAVE TOWN. Main Street, in Hopkinsville, portrayed this appearance about the time Edgar Cayce and his family moved from Hopkinsville to Selma, Alabama in 1912. This scene looking north on Main from Ninth Street revealed the Holland's Opera House building, at right, and the upstairs office of Dr. Al Layne, at left.

East 9th Street, Hopkinsville,

THE ROUTE EAST. This image in 1910 showed East Ninth Street from Main Street and was the route taken by travelers east to Russellville, Kentucky and south to Nashville, Tennessee. Edgar worked in the photographic studio of W.R. Bowles, noted in this picture by the sidewalk awnings at left. A summertime custom called for water wagons to daily spray the rock streets, with each business owner paying a monthly fee for this service.

A BUSY DAY. Storefront awnings, two-story brick business houses, and rock streets greeted shoppers in downtown Hopkinsville circa 1906. Businesses along the route familiar to Edgar Cayce were J.H. Anderson Dry Goods, F.A. Yost Hardware Company, the Hopkinsville Kentuckian office, First National Bank, Anderson-Fowler Drug Store, and the Phoenix Hotel.

MAIN FROM ELEVENTH AND BEYOND. Sparse telephone poles and very limited traffic punctuated this circa 1905 streetscape of downtown's Main Street looking north. The Ragsdale-Cooper office building and tobacco warehouse occupied the block, later where the popular restaurant, Ferrell's, is located at left and facing the Hille flats – rented rooms, and the Forbes Hardware at right.

NIGHT RIDER DESTRUCTION. In the pre-dawn hours of Saturday morning, December 7, 1907, five hundred masked farmers, called Night Riders, raided Hopkinsville and burned three tobacco warehouses. This view shows the southwest corner of Ninth and Campbell Streets were two of the warehouses were burned. The country rearing of Edgar Cayce, when dark tobacco prices were severely low, gave him a full understanding when farmers took the law into their own hands to fight the Duke tobacco trust.

CHAPTER

4

DOWNTOWN ENTERTAINMENT

TRADING DAY IN TOWN. A large crowd gathered in what the chamber of commerce called the "Dimple of the Pennyroyal" on trade day in 1908. This event brought men and boys to swap pocketknives, marbles, and watch fobs as well as to trade mules, beeswax, and food products. This image showed the crowd on Main Street, looking north at the Ninth Street intersection.

ANIMALS IN THE STREET! The era of circus parades and tent shows illustrated a popular attraction for great crowds of people before automobiles and radio. This scene featured the elephant line of Buffalo Bill's Wild West Shows as it marched south on Main Street in front of Holland's Opera House in October, 1901.

ELEPHANTS, DOGS, AND STEPPING STONES. Edgar Cayce captured this scene at the corner of South Virginia and 14th Streets in October, 1901. The home, in right background, was long the residence of Edgar's beloved uncle and aunt, Clint and Lula Boyd Cayce. The parade was beginning its march toward downtown Hopkinsville.

A RARE SIGHT. The time was October, 1901. The place was 14th Street between Main and Virginia Streets. The event illustrates the show steam-powered calliope drawn by eight white horses. The landmark is a rare side view of the First Baptist Church, built in 1894 and torn down in 1965.

FASHIONABLE MEN. Edgar Cayce's attention was peaked as he walked along the streets looking for a candid photograph. He found this couple, both men, one dressed as a woman, in the process of entertaining the crowd. The overhead banner advertised Buffalo Bill's World's Warriors who put on a show in Hopkinsville on October 4, 1901. This scene was on Main Street in front of the Phoenix Hotel.

A DAY OF PATRIOTISM. The intersection of Ninth and Main Streets, looking south, revealed a crowd anticipating a street parade. Edgar Cayce clicked the camera lens to record this view for history from the wrought-iron balcony on the second floor of the Holland's Opera House building. The Racket Store sign appeared on the roof, at left, and the Royal Saloon anchors the southwest corner of Ninth and Main Streets.

GET YOUR LIKENESS STRUCK. The Holland Opera House building provided a back drop for a Main Street carnival scene circa 1900. As an illegible banner hung from above, a customer could get his picture made in one-half minute by electricity for ten cents. Street carnivals were a huge attraction to young people when Edgar Cayce was of that age.

TRAPEZE IN THE STREET. The first street fair in Hopkinsville, October, 1899, featured a trapeze show with the equipment poles occupying pre-dug holes for the occasion. This view, looking north across the Ninth and Main Streets intersection, featured canvas banners from the Spanish-American War.

ELKS CLUB PARADE AND BEAUTY CONTEST. This 1900 scene portrayed the float of beauty contestants in the B.P.O.E. event originating in 1900 and continuing for several years. The annual event created a great amount of community interest. The camera was set up on Virginia Street facing the side of the American Express Company at its Ninth Street office, later the site of Tom Wade's Men's Store.

LADIES ALL DECKED OUT. The cameraman in the previous picture moved only a few feet to photograph four Hopkinsville belles all decked out in an open carriage and awaiting the beginning of the parade. The young boys on horses were escorts. W.R. Bowles photographic studio was located on the second floor in the building behind the art gallery sign. Note the roof profile of the old two-story log house, which stood on the northeast corner of Ninth and Virginia Streets.

SECOND FLOOR PARADE VIEW. A photographer leaned out of a second story window on Main Street, opposite the courthouse, and shot into permanent view a parade scene looking south across the Seventh Street intersection. Note the rare presence of an automobile in this circa 1910 picture.

CHAPTER

5

LANDMARK LEGACIES
IN THE MIND OF CAYCE

HUFFMAN'S MILL. Edgar Cayce's boyhood experiences included trips to the water mill where the miller, charging a one-eighth toll, ground the farm produced wheat into flour and corn into corn meal. There he gathered community news which he took home to the family. This mill, constructed on Little River near Edgar's birthplace, was operated by William B. Mason and later by Phil P. Huffman during the time he made visits there. The mill closed circa 1910 and was torn down in the spring of 1937 following the big flood.

IN RARE VIEW. The collection of scenes of county water mill portrayed the images from the river side. This photograph features Huffman's Mill, which stood for a century following its construction in 1837. The bridge, shown at right, was used to deliver corn and wheat to the second floor level of the mill. Occasional flooding of Little River caused the shut down of the milling operation. Neighborhood farmer, John Tom Adams, in his Sunday suit, stands by the remnant of an old buggy.

WORD'S STORE AT BEVERLY. The country store, churches, the one-room school and the water mill served as the foundation for community social and business life in the childhood of Edgar Cayce. Country men gathered here to share the news, vote, receive the weekly mail delivery, and buy the few staple goods not provided in farm production. His father, Leslie B. Cayce, was merchant and post-master in a store on this site from 1877 until 1879. That store burned on July 18, 1914 and was replaced by the present structure.

ROUTE TO THE WORLD. Edgar first saw an iron horse, fueled by coal, baggage and passenger cars, mail order catalog merchandise, and people coming and going in an era when travel was hindered by muddy and dusty roads. The L&N Railroad Station, at Herndon, Kentucky, built in 1886, was a draw to the imagination of a nine year old boy when it was completed. The last train run on this line was made on May 13, 1933 and the station was torn down in 1945, the year of Edgar Cayce's death.

EARLY VIEW OF THE COURTHOUSE. Edgar Cayce's photo collection revealed this view of the courthouse. Stone walls, log cabins with rock chimneys, and the first cupola show the earliest known photograph of this landmark. Completed in 1869, at a cost of $100,000, and designed by Evansville architect, Joseph K. Frick, the structure replaced the courthouse which was burned by C.S.A. General Hylan B. Lyon on December 12, 1864.

A TRIAL THAT NEVER HAPPENED. This image of the Christian County courthouse shows the building as it was at the time of a strain on the psychic life of Edgar Cayce. In 1910, Edgar formed the Psychic Reading Corporation with Dr. Wesley Ketchum, Albert D. Noe, Sr., and Leslie B. Cayce. They established a first class photographic studio for him in return for a division of the funds derived from Cayce's psychic readings. Cayce filed suit against them for $28,000 in Christian Circuit Court for breach of contract. The case, which would have been tried in this building, was settled out of court in March, 1913.

WHERE IT ALL BEGAN. The place was the stage of Holland's Opera House on Main Street in February, 1901. The event was the performance of a magician billed as "Hart, The Laugh Man." The performer called upon 23 year old Edgar Cayce to come to the stage and submit to a hypnotic trance. Having lost his voice in April, 1900, by the power of suggestion, the command was made for his voice to return. Before a shocked audience of 700 people, the miracle took place. There is no surviving photograph of that event. The portrayed image of the stage featured a home talent show in 1895.

A STAGE FOR NATIONAL PERFORMERS. The Methodist evangelist, Sam Jones of Atlanta, Georgia, ignited a flame which led to the construction of this civic auditorium in 1893. The 2000 seat facility was built at a cost of $4200. Located on the southeast corner of West Seventh Street and Cleveland Avenue, it was here that Edgar Cayce heard national figures including Dwight L. Moody, Theodore Roosevelt, John Phillip Sousa and his band, Booker T. Washington, and William Jennings Bryan. This landmark was torn down in 1941.

NINTH STREET NIGHT SPOT. The last years of Edgar Cayce's residency in Hopkinsville included the construction and opening of the Princess Theatre. In operation from 1911 until 1972, this site featured the first showing of "talking pictures' in Hopkinsville. Edgar and Gertrude may have occasionally frequented this movie house.

WESTERN KENTUCKY LUNATIC ASYLUM. Hopkinsville's largest 19th century employer was the mental hospital located on the Russellville Road. Established in 1848, and opened in 1854, the building was constructed by Gertrude's grandfather, Samuel L. Salter, and his contracting partner, John Orr. After its destruction by fire on November 30, 1860, Salter reconstructed the hospital and continued to serve as its building superintendent until his death in 1897.

ODD FELLOW'S BUILDING. An anchor landmark in downtown Hopkinsville is this structure located on the northeast corner of East Ninth and Virginia Streets. The lodge, formed in 1848, constructed this building in 1902. L.A. Johnson's Drug Store, with its popular soda fountain, was a favorite stop for young people in the later years Edgar Cayce lived in Hopkinsville.

HOPKINSVILLE SANITARIUM. Dr. Charles B. Petrie opened the first medical hospital in Hopkinsville on the northeast corner of Seventh and Clay Streets in November, 1905. James L. Long was the architect for this 60x40 foot building with an operating room and 13 patient rooms. Few area residents made use of the facility and it closed in 1909.

ENTRANCE TO HOPKINSVILLE. Throughout Edgar Cayce's life, the site of this landmark was the indication that he was home. Constructed in 1892, the station was framed with weatherboarding. In 1909, the stucco surface was applied and a 280-foot-long-trackside-covered shed was built and extended from Ninth to Eleventh Streets. It was here that Dr. Hugo Munsterberg, from Harvard University, arrived to investigate Edgar Cayce and took passage in Uncle Billy Evans' hack out to "The Hill", the Salter home on East Seventh Street, where Edgar Cayce was then residing.

TICKET TO ANYWHERE. The traveling public entered the ticket office of the L&N Railroad Passenger Depot, located on East Ninth Street, to buy their ticket to see the world. Honeymoon trips, sight seeing excursions, trips to the World's Fairs, and general business and pleasure trips originated by buying tickets in this room. Edgar Cayce often made use of this facility during his visits back to his home town.

I.C.R.R & T.C.R.W. PASSENGER STATION. Travelers arriving and departing Hopkinsville, for points south and west, used this landmark, located on the southwest corner of West Ninth and Bethel Streets. Both the Illinois Central and the Tennessee Central used this station, constructed in 1892, and torn down in 1942. Edgar Cayce's family used this station for trips to Cerulean Springs, Paducah, and other western destinations.

HERE COME THE FIRE WAG-
ONS. (left) The hourly striking of
the town clock fire bell, from its
eighty-five foot high tower, which
was used for the drying of fire hose,
was a familiar and loving sound to
Edgar Cayce. The Central Fire Station, designed by W.A. Long and
constructed in 1904-1905, was a key
figure in the Hopkinsville skyline
until it was destroyed by fire on October 3-4, 1924.

ROCK BRIDGE. (below) Contrac-
tor, William Hyde constructed the
Rock Bridge over the town fork of
Little River on North Main Street
near the south entrance to Riverside
Cemetery in 1858. The one-lane
stone structure became a well-known
landmark before it was intentionally
dynamited in 1907 for the construction of an iron bridge. Edgar Cayce
made many trips over this bridge
when attending the burial of family
members and friends.

THERE IT STANDS ON THE HILL. On January 8, 1896, two years after Edgar Cayce had moved to Hopkinsville, the city installed a public water works system. The 107 foot high stand pipe with a capacity of 234,960 gallons, located on Gainesville Hill, near East First Street, provided the pressure to supply the city with an ample water supply. It was removed in December, 1974 to be replaced by a two million gallon tank.

HARNESSING THE WATER SUPPLY. The Hopkinsville Water Works Dam, located on the town fork of Little River, northeast of Hopkinsville, has provided a pool of water for the pumping station since 1895. Constructed of stone and concrete, it reveals little change after over 110 years. The mill pond created by the dam was the site of many fishing and swimming trips by Edgar Cayce.

THE BRIDGE TO COURTSHIP. The West Seventh Street stone double-arched bridge connecting downtown Hopkinsville with the west side of town was a familiar landmark to Edgar Cayce. Constructed by William Hyde in 1882, the bridge was situated along the route Edgar Cayce took on foot or bicycle as he traveled Seventh Street to "The Hill" to court Gertrude. This scene illustrated the effects of an ice storm in 1901.

SITE OF EARLY READINGS. Constructed in 1905, the downtown office of Dalton Bros. Brick Company stands on the southwest corner of Virginia and Seventh Streets. Dr. Wesley H. Ketchum, who claimed to have "discovered" Edgar Cayce, had his office on the second floor. Hotel Latham stood across the street from this building.

THE RECEPTION ROOM. The waiting room of the office of the homeopathic physician, Dr. Wesley H. Ketchum, is the feature of this image. It was located on the second floor of the Dalton Building from 1905 until 1912. Edgar Cayce gave a number of psychic readings at this location.

A MARK OF DISTINCTION. In 1970, the Kentucky Historical Society and the Kentucky Department of Highways erected this state highway historical marker at the main entrance of Riverside Cemetery on North Main Street. It is the only informational monument portraying the life of Edgar Cayce in Hopkinsville.

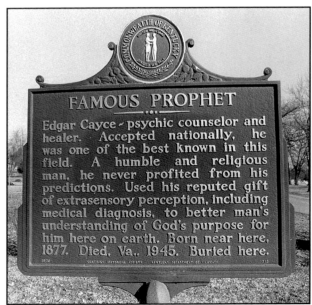

CHAPTER

6

PILLARS OF INFLUENCE
IN THE LIFE OF EDGAR CAYCE

GOSPEL ADVOCATE. Granville Lipscomb was minister of Liberty Christian Church, 1887-1889. It was during his ministry that Edgar Cayce made a profession of faith and joined the church on October 13, 1888. He was baptized in the pond of his great uncle, Jim Cayce, near Little River at Hargis' Bridge. Edgar's first job in the church was to serve as janitor and to build fires in the two coal stoves every Sunday morning. He would later serve as Sunday School Superintendent. The foundation of his faith, which was laid at old Liberty Church, would serve as the anchor of his life.

QUININE JIM. The year Edgar Cayce was born U.S. Congressman, from this district, James A. McKenzie made a speech on the floor of the House calling for the removal of a tariff on quinine, the principle medicine given to children when suffering from the chills. The high tariff limited the use of this medicine. McKenzie's speech was so effective that the quinine tariff was lowered. Thirteen years later, Edgar, a student at Beverly Academy, committed to memory the one-hour, ten minute speech and delivered it without the use of notes before a large crowd gathered at the school.

THE OLD SCHOOLMASTER. Professor Bernardino Emelio "B.E." Thom was Edgar Cayce's beloved school teacher at Beverly Academy, 1889-1890. Professor Thom recognized his pupil's limited capability when he found the boy at age 13 in the third grade. The professor's understanding, interest, and motivation awakened Edgar to the pursuit of knowledge through reading. Though the schoolmaster did not comprehend Cayce's gift of psychic clairvoyance, he served as a constant source of support. Years later, when they both lived in Virginia, Cayce and Thom were in frequent contact.

TOWN MINISTERS. Edgar Cayce moved to Hopkinsville in 1894 and soon moved his church membership to the Ninth Street Christian Church. The minister was J.W. Mitchell, top image, who served from 1892 to 1896 and was followed by Harry D. Smith, bottom image. Smith served the congregation for 18 years and was very effective in his ministry and pastorate. It was during the years prior to 1902, when Edgar moved to Bowling Green, that he taught a boy's Sunday school class at the church.

TABERNACLE BUILDER. Edgar Cayce was greatly influenced by the preaching of the Methodist evangelist Sam Jones of Atlanta. The four revivals conducted by Jones in Hopkinsville led to the construction of Union Tabernacle, a 2500 seat brick auditorium. The community civic center was constructed in 1893 on the southeast corner of West Seventh and Cleveland Avenue. Other evangelists included Dwight L. Moody, Mordichai F. Ham, Burke Culpepper, and Wade House.

19th CENTURY BILLY GRAHAM. One morning at dawn in September, 1899, Edgar Cayce drove a cow to pasture at Dry Branch, behind Cayce's Pharmacy today, from his West Seventh Street home. There he found sitting on a log and meditating, the most famous and highly respected evangelist in the United States, Dwight L. Moody. The two struck up a conversation and 22 year old Cayce discussed with him his desire to become a minister. Edgar attended the one-week Moody Revival at the Union Tabernacle, located on southeast corner of West Seventh and Cleveland Avenue.

A FRIEND TO SECRET SERVICE. The young manhood years Edgar spent in Hopkinsville led to a lifelong friendship with Colonel Will Starling, later a member of the White House Secret Service detail. Forty years passed between that youthful relationship when Edgar served the President of the United States, Woodrow Wilson, through psychic readings from his contact with Colonel Will.

A HELPING HAND. In the spring of 1900, Edgar Cayce lost his voice. After taking a business course in Louisville, Kentucky, he returned to Hopkinsville and was offered a job in the photographic studio of William R. Bowles. There he would work for two years and master from the teaching of "Uncle Billy", as he was known, the art of photography. Though Edgar was involved in several other business pursuits during his life, he always returned to his first professional love, the art of capturing the moment through photographs.

ANOTHER OPPORTUNITY. In 1902, then Hopkinsville merchant, Frank H. Bassett obtained for Edgar Cayce a photographers position in Bowling Green, Kentucky with Lucian D. Potter's Book Store. Two years later, Edgar formed a photographic studio partnership with Frank J. Potter. His experience at Bowles Studio in Hopkinsville, along with Bassett's friendship, opened his world of interest in the photographic business.

PERSONALITIES AT PILOT ROCK. A group of people, strong in their influence on Edgar Cayce, are gathered for a picnic near Pilot Rock in 1901. This popular picnic point is located northeast of Hopkinsville on the Butler Road at the Christian County, Todd County line. About to consume a bounty of food, the group includes, from left, Mrs. Charles H. Hisgen, John Hisgen, Estella Smith, Albert Hisgen, Sarah Dillman, Gertrude Evans and Edgar Cayce.

THE YANKEE PROFESSOR. In 1883, one year
after the establishment of the Hopkinsville City
School System, the school board employed a new
Superintendent, Charles H. Dietrich from Freder-
icksburg, Ohio. His tenure of service established
an outstanding school operation. Dietrich married
a local young lady, Minnie Lander, and they were
the parents of "Little Amie" who contributed a
very important early chapter in Edgar Cayce's
medical readings.

A PHYSICIAN'S SUPPORT. Hopkinsville physician, Dr. Thomas Burr House, at right, was
one of the first members of the medical profession to endorse Edgar's work. Years later, he
would serve in the role of physician at the Virginia Beach Hospital. Edgar Cayce, at left, and
Raymond Smith, center, Gertrude's cousin, joined the doctor in this pose.

MEDICAL PIONEER PATIENT. On May 31, 1905, George Dalton, co-owner of Dalton Bros. Brickyard, sustained a broken leg above and below the kneecap while surveying the construction site of L&N Railroad Freight Depot on East Ninth Street. After consulting with several doctors, the family called upon Dr. Wesley H. Ketchum, another local physician, who used Edgar Cayce readings to treat Dalton. Psychic medical readings prescribed the use of a blacksmith-fashioned nail driven into the kneecap and the use of weights extended over the foot of the bed to create traction for the injured knee. These techniques were pioneer efforts in the medical profession. The patient recovered and lived another 17 years.

BUSINESS PROMOTER. Albert D. Noe, Sr., owner and operator of Hopkinsville's Hotel Latham, was another individual who attempted financial gain from Edgar Cayce's gift. In 1910, he joined Ketchum and L.B. Cayce to establish a business arrangement by which he would receive one-third of the profit derived from the psychic readings. This business relationship collapsed when the partners misused Edgar's talent.

DRUGGIST FOR MEDICAL READINGS. Professional medical opposition of filling psychic reading prescriptions created a problem for Edgar Cayce. One of the few druggists who would cooperate was the beloved local personality, Max J. Blythe. He worked at Cook & Higgins Drug Store, located on the west side of Main Street between Seventh and Court Streets.

THE YANKEE DOCTOR. One of the more significant physicians in the psychic work of Edgar Cayce was Dr. Wesley H. Ketchum, at left. A native of Lisben, Ohio, and a graduate of the Cleveland Homeopathic Medical College, he located his practice in Hopkinsville in 1904 and became a very well-respected physician. In 1910, Dr. Ketchum prepared a paper on Edgar Cayce which was presented before the Boston Medical Society. His son Alton, at right, was an advertising designer and in later years contributed a number of artifacts to the local Pennyroyal Area Museum.

NEIGHBORHOOD FRIEND. Edgar and Gertrude Cayce lived on South Main Street from 1910 until 1912. An across the street neighbor, Dr. J.E. Stone was a friend and supporter of Edgar Cayce as he struggled to determine the course and direction of his life concerning the psychic gift.

A CASE STUDY. The scene is the family sitting room in the home of school superintendent, Charles H. and Minnie Dietrich on South Walnut Street. The year was circa 1902 and includes from left, the Dietrich children, Karl, Amie, and Lois. Amie, who suffered from stunted growth because of a fall on a carriage step, was prescribed, through a medical reading by Edgar, low grade electrical impulses by wet cell appliances to her spine. After treatment, Amie was cured

CHAPTER

7

EDGAR CAYCE: THE PHOTOGRAPHER

W.R. BOWLES PHOTOGRAPHIC STUDIO. In 1900, Edgar Cayce lost his voice. Unable to continue working as an insurance salesman, he obtained a job in the photographic studio of William R. Bowles. Uncle Billy, as he was affectionately known, operated the principle photographic studio at that time. His photo gallery was located on the second floor of the Chickasaw building, located on the northwest corner of East Ninth and Virginia Streets. During the two years Cayce worked here, he not only discovered the niche which would become his life's professional work but he also came to exhibit a tremendous talent in getting people to pose for photographs.

EDGAR CAYCE STUDIO. In 1912, Albert D. Noe, Sr., Dr. Wesley H. Ketchum, and Leslie B. Cayce established a first-class photographic studio for Edgar Cayce. It was located on the second floor of the Thompson building, located on the east side of South Main Street between Seventh and Eighth Streets. Many psychic readings were given at this location during the two years in which he worked. This landmark was destroyed by fire on December 31, 1984.

THREE TIME CANDIDATE. The location was at the intersection of Ninth and Main Streets in downtown Hopkinsville. In October, 1899, former and future Democratic candidate for United States President, William Jennings Bryan was photographed by Edgar Cayce. Bryan was speaking before a large crowd as he endorsed the candidacy of Democratic candidate, William Goebel, as he campaigned for the office of Governor of the Commonwealth of Kentucky.

MOST FAMOUS PHOTOGRAPH. In October, 1900, the Republican candidate for United States Vice-President, Theodore Roosevelt came to Hopkinsville to speak during the Presidential campaign. Edgar Cayce captured this image of the "Rough Rider" as he left the carriage for his public address before a capacity crowd in Union Tabernacle.

AN ADMIRING COUPLE. Sometime during the period of their unofficial engagement, Edgar and Gertrude were photographed on the front porch at "The Hill. The East Seventh Street home of Gertrude's grandfather Salter in this snap of the camera lens, as with many others, Edgar has activated a bulb in one hand to expose the desired image.

WHILE OUT FOR A RIDE. Edgar and Gertrude enjoyed many buggy rides out through the countryside. Along the way, Edgar exercised the good judgment to pause and to photograph a number of county landmarks. On the day this scene was taken, the young couple had driven to Fairview, Kentucky, ten miles east of Hopkinsville, and there he recorded for posterity a picture of Bethel Baptist Church. This church, still standing, was built in 1886 on the site of the birthplace of Confederate President, Jefferson Davis.

FROZEN IN TIME: A century ago, fraternal organizations were very popular across the United States. One of those groups in Hopkinsville was the Pearl City Lodge #5, Woodmen of the World, a nationwide insurance organization. It was chartered on December 30, 1898. The group promoted and supported civic, family, charitable, and patriotic activities. Edgar is pictured, top row second from right, as he squeezes the bulb to capture the image. His father, Leslie B. Cayce is standing on the back row, at left, under the flag. Some of the other men in this pose included John R. Kitchen, John B. Galbreath, Dr. J.B. Jackson, James D. Russell, Hunter Wood, Jr., Lucian H. Davis, John W. Harned, Andrew J, Meador, Ike Hart, Joe D. Higgins, J.E. Claiborne, Archie Higgins, William T. Fowler, Will E. Williamson, George D. Dalton, and E.H. Higgins.

CHAPTER

8

FAMILY HOMES

CEDAR GROVE. Edgar Cayce's mother, Carrie Major Cayce, was born in this home, located .08 of a mile south of Beverly, on June 23, 1855. There, she married Leslie Burr Cayce on June 10, 1874. The brick story and a half house was built circa 1817 by Toliver Bronaugh and later served as the residence of ministers of the Presbyterian congregation in that neighborhood. In the 1850s, a two-story frame section with a double portico was added to the west end of the house. This section was removed in the 1920s. Carrie's father and mother, Uriah Lodowick Major and Elizabeth Ann Sergeant Major lived here through the mid-19th-century. The land-

mark was later occupied by their son, Thomas H. Major and his wife, Mary Killen Major and then by their daughter, Katherine Major and her husband, R.H. Swift. The home has been extensively remodeled by Travis and Jenny Askew, the present occupants.

COTTAGE ON BIRTHPLACE SITE. Today the crumbling remains of a two-room cottage, located south of Beverly Store, with a double lean two, marks the birthplace site of Edgar Cayce. His mother inherited the 147 acre Robert Lewis farm from her father. The year Edgar was born his father mortgaged the farm to buy the stock of goods in Beverly Store. Deflated farm prices caused the loss of this farm and the new owner, John Dabney Jones, constructed the house in this image in 1879.

COTTAGE IN THE WOODS. The failure of the store business in 1879 forced the removal of Edgar's family to a two-room cottage, located on the farm of his grandfather, Tom Cayce. The 14 years Edgar resided here brought many experiences into his life. The imaginary playmates, the vision in the woods, and a personal witness of the deaths of his Cayce grandparents brought him into reality with many unexplainable thoughts concerning the "gift". This cottage, from the east and west, stood unoccupied until the mid-1960s.

OCCASIONAL VISITS. The boyhood years of Edgar Cayce were spent visiting homes and families of many relatives. The three featured were the homes of great-uncles in the Cayce family. The top image shows Locust Grove, the 343 acre farm home of his grandfather's brother, George Washington Cayce. Built in 1865, pictured in 1898, the landmark remains in the family today. The middle photograph portrays the 115 acre farm home of Franklin Pierce Cayce. It was constructed in circa 1857 using logs from the original Liberty Meeting House, built in 1814. The bottom picture reveals Oak Hill, the 400 acre farm home of James Monroe Cayce. It was constructed in the 1860s and was torn down circa 1949.

A FAMILY CONNECTION. Four and a half miles south of the courthouse at Hopkinsville, on the Palmyra, now Lafayette, Road, stands the Robert Cayce home. It was constructed in 1878 by his father, George Roy Cayce, a first cousin of Edgar Cayce's father. Robert and his wife, Loula Cayce, maintained a letter correspondence with his famous Virginia cousin during the 1930s on the genealogy of the family. Labor Day weekend of 1935 witnessed a large Cayce family reunion which was attended by Edgar.

EDGAR'S FIRST HOPKINSVILLE HOME. A log two-story house to which Edgar's family moved in December, 1893 is located on the southeast corner of West Seventh and Young Streets. This landmark was one of several homes rented by the Les Cayce family, during their over 30 year residency, in Hopkinsville.

PRE-CIVIL WAR LANDMARK. Another West Side home, the R.L. Boulware house, occupied by the Les Cayce family stood on the future site of West Side School. Edgar Cayce captured these scenes, the second probably his bedroom, before the house was torn down prior to 1905.

SITE OF FIRST PSYCHIC READING. Now known as the J.T. Walker place, at 530 West Seventh Street, the Les Cayce family was residing here on March 30, 1901 at the time of the first psychic reading. The reading was conducted in the dining room of this landmark home.

THE HILL. The house which played the most important role in the Edgar Cayce story was the Salter home, located on East Seventh Street. Edgar Cayce and Gertrude Evans were married there by the Christian Church minister Harry D. Smith on June 17, 1903. It was to this home, built by Gertrude's grandfa-

ther Samuel L. Salter, they returned for many visits throughout the next 40 years. Fire destroyed the structure on December 2, 1964.

THE COTTAGE. For a brief time in the fall of 1909, Edgar, Gertrude, and Hugh Lynn lived in a small house owned by Gertrude's aunts on East Seventh Street. It was to this home that Dr. Hugo Munsterberg, of Harvard University, came to investigate Edgar Cayce's psychic gift.

ARNOLD COTTAGE. From October, 1910, until March, 1912, the Edgar Cayce family resided in this home, owned by Mrs. Caroline Webber Arnold, at 1910 South Main Street. Here, their second son Milton Porter Cayce was born on March 28 and died on May 17, 1911. The family moved from this location to Anniston, Alabama and then to Selma.

310 WEST 15th STREET. Les and Carrie Cayce and their daughters lived near Bethel Woman's College during the era of World War I. Les was engaged in photography, Carrie was a seamstress, and the daughters were sales ladies in downtown stores.

DURRETT HOMESTEAD. The last Hopkinsville home, the R.T. Durrett place, occupied by the Les Cayce family, stood on the northeast corner of South Walnut Street and Maple Court. Daughter, Annie Cayce was operating her millinery store in the Pennyroyal Apartments building. The other daughters had married or moved out of town and Les was living with Edgar's family in Virginia Beach, Virginia. Edgar's mother, Carrie died here on October 26, 1926.

THE DIETRICH PLACE. The Yankee professor, Charles H. Dietrich, his wife Minnie, and their three children Karl, Amie, and Lois resided here when the professor was superintendent of the city schools and later a salesman for the American Book Company. To this home came Edgar Cayce to apply the treatment prescribed in his readings for Amie. In 1902, treatment proved successful and Amie was cured.

KEIGHTLEY FUNERAL HOME. Edgar Cayce's funeral was conducted in this landmark home on January 5, 1945. Gertrude's services followed on April 3, 1945. It was constructed in 1852 by Baptist minister Achilles DeGrasse Sears and later became the home of prominent residents Stephen E. Trice and J. Waller Downer. The structure is now the site of Ann's Tea Room

CHAPTER

9

PULPITS AND BLACKBOARDS

LIBERTY CHRISTIAN CHURCH. Edgar Cayce joined this church in 1888 and was baptized in his great-uncle Jim Cayce's pond. The congregation was established in 1840 with this frame building erected in 1856. It stood on the Palmyra, now Lafayette, Road, south of Hopkinsville, and was replaced by the present structure in 1952. After serving as sexton of the church, Cayce became Sunday School Superintendent. While visiting in Hopkinsville in the summer of 1942, he made his last visit to this site of his early religious experience.

CHURCH GATHERING. The congregation at Liberty Church assembled for a group photograph during a revival circa 1888. Evangelist William Y. Stanley is shown standing, at right, with minister John T. Hawkins sitting, at left, and members of the Pace, Major, Cayce, Stroube, Childress, and Killebrew families standing and sitting.

LOCUST GROVE BAPTIST CHURCH. In 1842, members of the Salem Baptist Church organized this church at a location near their homes. Edgar Cayce's maternal grandparents, Uriah Lodowich "U.L" Major and his wife Elizabeth Ann Seargeant Major were charter members. Their daughter Carrie, Edgar's mother, was later a member here. The present church was constructed in 1857 and has remained relatively unchanged since that time.

EDGAR'S TOWN CHURCH. Ninth Street Christian Church in Hopkinsville was established in 1832. In 1850, the congregation constructed the Gothic style structure, top image, located on northwest corner of Ninth and Liberty Streets. South Kentucky College operated in the lower level of this building from 1850 until 1858. The church was remodeled and enlarged, opposite page top image, in 1907. The image below, features the sanctuary after the remodeling in 1887 with the addition of an air bellows powered church pipe organ. That action led to a division in the church out of which developed the Church of Christ at another location. Edgar Cayce was a member here from 1894 until 1912. This landmark was demolished in 1958 when the congregation moved to South Walnut Street and Morningside Drive.

CHRISTIAN CHURCH, HOPKINSVILLE, KY.

The Ninth Street Christian Church, above, after remodeling in 1907.

NINTH STREET METHODIST CHURCH. Before and after remodeling images portray this Hopkinsville landmark, located on the southwest corner of East Ninth and Clay Streets. Gertrude Evans, later the wife of Edgar Cayce, was a member of this congregation in young womanhood. This first picture shows the church as it was constructed in 1848. The second view revealed the results after the remodeling in 1892. The building was torn down in 1919.

BEVERLY ACADEMY. This country school, located in the Beverly community on the Old Palmyra Road, was attended by Edgar Cayce from 1889 until 1893. This significant period in his life was revealed through his spelling book experience and the reciting of "Quinine Jim" McKenzie's speech on tariff removal on the floor of the United States House of Representatives.

BEVERLY ACADEMY SCHOLARS. On November 25, 1890, Hopkinsville photographer Clarence Anderson snapped the shutter and perpetuated for all time the faces of teachers and scholars of Beverly Academy. The six people on the left side of the picture are Isaac Cayce, Mrs. Cayce (Miss Jo), the teacher, George Major, trustee Eugene Word, Will Major, and Edgar Cayce. First row, from left, contains Hugh Major, Fenton Cayce, Harry Childress, Mammie Radford, Ruth Major, Lessie Bradshaw, Alta Kenner, Maude Baker, Mary Cayce (Edgar's sister), Fred Moss (on knees), teacher B.E. Thom, and trustee Leslie B. Cayce (Edgar's father). In the second row are Eugene Word, Jennie Major, Iva Cayce, Aubrey Major, Fulton Major, Oscar Hargis, Wesley Johnson, Perry Johnson, _____ Hargis, Hendricks Major, Roy Cayce, Campbell Moss, Rob Kenner, Brenda Kenner, Lizzie Major, and Charlie Major. On the back row was Richard Pace, Beckie Hargis, Ben West, Junius Cayce, Mary Lou Kenner, Charlie Cayce, Pearl Cayce, Roy Kenner, Will Davis (in window), Bessie Kenner, Walter Word, Annie Cayce (Edgar's sister), George Steger, Addie Major, John Major, Ann Hargis, Bird Carter, Ola Cayce (Edgar's sister), and Jim Bradshaw.

BEVERLY ACADEMY INTERIOR. After 90 years of use as a corn crib, equipment storage shed, tenant house, and artifact storage for the Pennyroyal Area Museum, Beverly Academy once again was returned to the appearance of its original use. In 1999-2000, the co-authors removed debris, painted, and with the help of carpenters, restored the building and the community celebrated its completion with a ribbon cutting and open house on September 24, 2000. Over 300 people attended the event. Today, the Pennyroyal Area Museum conducts educational class sessions and provides late-19th century games for elementary students throughout the area.

CLAY STREET SCHOOL. This grade and high school, located on the east side of Clay Street between Fourth and Fifth Streets, served as the city's white public grade and high school from 1881 until 1912. Gertrude Evans, Edgar Cayce's future wife, attended this school as a young lady. The building was torn down in 1915 and the brick and stone were used in the construction of Attucks High School.

SOUTH KENTUCKY COLLEGE. This view reveals the college when Gertrude Evans was a student there in the early 1890s. Organized in 1849, on Belmont Hill, as a girl's school by the Christian churches of Western Kentucky and Western Tennessee, it became co-educational in 1881. The name was changed to McLean College in 1908. It closed and merged with Transylvania College in 1914. Fires destroyed the main building in 1884, 1905, and 1912.

THE PREP SCHOOL. South Kentucky College prep school students were photographed on the front porch of the college circa 1890. Miss Mary Green was the teacher and Gertrude Evans is identified by the arrow.

GERTRUDE'S CLASSMATES. The Physics class at South Kentucky College appeared in their best clothing for a photograph in front of the school in 1895. College group pictures in Hopkinsville are rare finds over a century later. Gertrude Evans is seated in front row, center.

GERTRUDE'S ALMA MATER DESTROYED. On November 2, 1905, less than ten years after Gertrude Evans, the future wife of Edgar Cayce, attended school here, it was destroyed by fire. This Christian Church supported, co-educational college was in operation for 55 years and was located on Belmont Hill.

CHAPTER

10

FAMILY TIES

Elizabeth "Betsey" Garret Cayce

Mary "Polly" Gary Seargeant

EDGAR'S GREAT-GRANDMOTHERS. (opposite page) Edgar Cayce's love for photography can truly be portrayed in the images of two of his great-grandmothers, both born in the 18th-century. Each attained the age of 80 and both of these women moved from Virginia to settle in Christian County in the early 19th-century. These photographs feature the emerging art of photography 25 years after its development. Elizabeth "Betsey" Garret Cayce, far left image, paternal great-grandmother, was born in Buckingham County, Virginia on May 5, 1787. She married William Cayce there on May 3, 1806. They then moved to Montgomery County, Tennessee in 1817 and settled on Raccoon Creek, in what is now the Ft. Campbell military reservation. They moved to Christian County circa 1827 and settled on a farm near present Locust Grove Baptist Church. They had ten children; the youngest was Thomas Jefferson Cayce, grandfather of Edgar. Betsey Garret Cayce died on that farm, April 2, 1869. Mary "Polly" Gary Seargeant, near left image, maternal great-grandmother, was born in Buckingham County, Virginia on July 3, 1789. She married Andrew Harrison Seargeant circa 1812. They settled in Christian County at Cedar Grove, on the Palmyra Road, in 1833. Their daughter, Elizabeth Seargeant Major was the grandmother of Edgar Cayce. Polly Gary Seargeant died on August 20, 1869.

EDGAR'S GREAT-GREAT UNCLES. Edgar Cayce maintained a great interest in old family photographs. The two images shown are of men he never saw, but because they were direct relatives and their pictures survived, they are relevant to include. The men, brothers of Edgar's paternal great-grandmother, Elizabeth "Betsey" Garret Cayce lived in the Longview neighborhood near their sister. Isaac Garrott, Sr. (1792-1868),left image, was a very successful farmer and road builder. Pleasant Garrott (1802-1875), right image, was also a farmer and, along with his brother, was a member of Salem Baptist Church.

EDGAR'S PATERNAL GRANDPARENTS. Thomas Jefferson "Tom" Cayce was born in Christian County Kentucky on May 16, 1829. A successful farmer and tobacco warehouseman, he married Sarah P. Thomas on May 15, 1851. She was born in Montgomery County, Tennessee on December 7, 1826. The second son of their ten children was Leslie Burr Cayce, father of Edgar. Tom and Sarah sat for these photographs in the studio of Hopkinsville photographer Ezra L. Foulks circa 1867. Edgar was present at the deaths of both of his grandparents. Tom accidentally drowned in a pond on the farm on June 8, 1881 and Sarah died on August 8, 1893 of an extended illness. The bottom image of Tom and Sarah Cayce was painted from the above photographs by his niece Alice Cayce Hill circa 1900.

EDGAR'S MATERNAL GRAND-PARENTS. Uriah Lodowich "U.L." Major was born in Madison County, Virginia on February 11, 1809. He was a farmer and married Elizabeth Ann Seargeant on October 1, 1838. She was born in Buckingham County, Virginia on July 23, 1821. Their seventh child, Carrie was the mother of Edgar Cayce. They resided at Cedar Grove, the home farm of Elizabeth's father and mother. U.L. Major died on September 21, 1861 and Elizabeth Seargeant Major died on October 19, 1875.

GEORGE WASHINGTON CAYCE (1807-1897). Edgar's paternal grandfather's oldest brother was a farmer, road surveyor, and tobacco warehouseman. He married Amanda Brooks, lived northeast of Beverly at Locust Grove, and was a member of Liberty Christian Church.

MARTHA CAYCE ADAMS (1809-1889). The paternal great-aunt of Edgar Cayce, Martha Adams, was married to farmer, Benjamin Adams. They were members of Liberty Christian Church and lived on Striped Bridge Road in Christian County.

ELIZABETH CAYCE ADAMS (1818-1883). Another great-aunt of Edgar, on the Cayce side of the family, was "Lizzie" Adams. She was the wife of John Adams, a brother of Benjamin Adams. Lizzie and John were members of Liberty Christian Church and lived on the Palmyra Road, now Lafayette Road, near the present Stadium of Champions.

ISAAC NEWTON CAYCE (1821-1895). Edgar's great-uncle, Ike, was the only member of the family in that generation to leave Christian County. The family, members of the Christian Church, lived on the Locust Grove Road, east of Swallow Springs. In 1871, with wife, Martha Ellen Graves Cayce, and their nine children, the Ike Cayce family moved by covered wagon to Coryell County, Texas.

FRANKLIN PIERCE CAYCE (1826-1903). Another of Edgar's great-uncles, named for a President, was also a farmer, a member of Liberty Christian Church, and with his family resided on the Palmyra Road, now Lafayette Road. Frank married Priscilla Simpson and they had three children.

JAMES MONROE CAYCE (1827-1916). The last of Edgar's paternal great-uncles was Jim Cayce. Also a member of Liberty Christian Church, he was married four times and owned the farm Oak Hill, located on Little River at Hargis' Bridge.

THE TOM AND SARAH CAYCE FAMILY. In the summer of 1896, the eight surviving children of Tom and Sarah, along with in-laws and six grandchildren, gathered in the parlor of their parent's home near Beverly for an image to record a farm family before the homeplace was sold. Back row, left to right, Robert E. Lee Cayce, Delbert D. Cayce, Mattie McKnight Cayce (wife of Lucian), Matthew Cayce, Clinton Cayce, Lucian M. Cayce, Lou Ella Cayce Jones, Leslie B. Cayce, and Edgar Cayce. Middle row, left to right, Lena Jones Wicks, Col. Edwin D. Jones (husband of Ella), Eddie Jones Smithson (daughter of Ella), Lula Boyd Cayce (wife of Clint), Kenneth Odin Cayce (son of Delbert D.), Rebecca Dillman Cayce (wife of Delbert D.), Durwood D. Cayce (son of Delbert D.), and Ida Major Cayce (wife of Edgar). Front row, left to right, Granville L. Cayce, Sr. (son of Clint), and Bertha Cayce (daughter of Delbert D.).

PAPA AND MAMA. Leslie Burr "Les" Cayce and his wife, Carrie Major Cayce, were, next to Gertrude, the greatest influence on the life of their son. Les Cayce, the second son of ten children of Tom and Sarah Cayce, was born northeast of Beverly on July 3, 1853. He was a farmer, country store keeper, postmaster from 1877-1879, insurance agent, photographer, and promoter of any opportunity that appeared to bring financial success. Les married Carrie Major on June 10, 1874. She was born on June 23, 1855, the third daughter and seventh child of

Uriah Lodowich Major and Elizabeth Ann Seargeant Major. Carrie attended Bethel Female College in Hopkinsville. In financial stress, Carrie operated a boarding house and was a domestic seamstress. Edgar was ever patient and loving with his unsettled father. The son's love for his mother was unconditional and he was devoted to the fulfillment of her every wish and need. Les Cayce died on April 11, 1937 in Nashville, Tennessee. Carrie died in Hopkinsville, Kentucky on October 26, 1926.

EDGAR'S NAMESAKE (1852-1927). The eldest child of Tom and Sarah Cayce was Edgar Cayce. Edgar's brother, Les, named his first born son for his older brother. The elder Edgar was a lifetime farmer on the Cox Mill Road and a member of Liberty Christian Church. He married Ida Major, a first cousin of Edgar's mother Carrie.

AUNT ELLA AND UNCLE ED.
Ella Cayce Jones (1855-1940) and her husband, farmer Edwin Dennis "Wildcat Ed" Jones, contributed an extensive influence on the life of Edgar Cayce. They lived in the Rich community, located KY 117 between Herndon and Newstead. Ella Jones was an attentive listener and supporter of Edgar throughout his experience with the "gift". Ed Jones, a Confederate veteran who was in General Lee's army at the surrender at Appomattox Courthouse, Virginia, settled in Christian County after the war and became a very successful farmer and community supporter. Ella and Ed were

liberal financial contributors to South Kentucky College, later McLean College.

THE FAMILY OF GREATEST SUPPORT. Edgar's uncle, Clinton H. "Clint" Cayce (1859-1942), a farmer, hardware merchant, and postmaster at Beverly Store in 1883, his wife, Lula Boyd Cayce, and their three children, from left to right, Maude Cayce Ryan, Florence Cayce, and Granville L. Cayce, Sr. were all very supportive of the "work". Financial support, a hardy welcome, and fellowship around a bountiful table were the hallmarks of this family's relationship to Edgar. A number of readings were given for the family.

THE BACHELOR UNCLE. Robert E. Lee Cayce (1863-1944), known simply as Uncle Lee, was somewhat a character in the Cayce family. A hardware merchant by trade and very successful businessman, he made and lost several fortunes. It is doubtful that his support of Edgar Cayce was ever positive.

THE RED TIE MAYOR. The most gregarious and colorful of Edgar's uncles was Lucian M. Cayce (1865-1936). His career included country store merchant and postmaster, teacher at Beverly Academy, salesman for Delker Buggy Company, Evansville, Indiana, and the fashionable red tie wearing Mayor of Hopkinsville, 1930-1934. His interest in nephew Edgar increased with the passing years.

HARDWARE MERCHANT UNCLE. Delbert D. Cayce, Sr. (1866-1927), longtime owner of Cayce-Yost Hardware Company on South Main Street in Hopkinsville, and his wife, Rebecca Dillman Cayce, were active in the community and members of Ninth Street Christian Church. Their children were very sociable to their cousin Edgar.

COUSINS AND FRIENDS. George Robert Cayce (1867-1960) and his wife, Loula Steger Cayce, maintained a longtime friendship with Edgar Cayce. Robert, ten years Edgar's senior, lived in the home neighborhood and also through the connection at Liberty Church cultivated an association that included assistance in family history research. Edgar's participation in several family reunions at their home developed a kinship association on his part to this extended family.

COUSIN TOM. Thomas Cayce "Tom" Jones (1876-1952) and his wife, Mattie Sue Browning Jones, generated an association through psychic readings with Tom's first cousin, Edgar Cayce. Tom owned the Tom C. Jones Insurance Agency, was a member of Ninth Street Christian Church, active in the Rotary Club, and one of the founders of the Hopkinsville Industrial Foundation.

COUSIN LENA. Lena Jones Wicks (1895-1985), business leader, soloist, choir director, genealogist, and political activist, launched the effort to make Hopkinsville aware of Edgar Cayce. She motivated the interest of a boy at age 14, co-author William T. Turner, to actively pursue a lifetime interest in local history, genealogy, and a knowledge of Edgar Cayce. A first cousin to Edgar, she was co-owner of Wicarson's Ladies Dress Shop. Through her efforts to preserve Riverside Chapel, she is considered "the mother of local historical preservation".

SARAH BEA MAJOR WEAVER (1801-1879). Aunt "Sallie" Weaver was Edgar's maternal grandfather's oldest sister. She married Jeremiah Weaver in Madison County, Virginia and they moved west in 1825 and settled in the Beverly neighborhood of south Christian County. Her father, Charles Major, and the rest of the family followed them to Christian County in 1826.

HOWARD MAJOR I (1811-1871). Edgar's maternal grandfather's younger brother was a farmer, blacksmith, and a strong advocate of the new Christian Church (Disciples of Christ) movement. He married Rachel McDonald and they lived on a part of his father's land, east of Beverly Store.

CHARLES HUMPHREY MAJOR (1817-1906). This maternal great-uncle of Edgar Cayce left home in 1836 to become a store clerk in Hopkinsville. In 1841, he moved to Trigg County and eventually owned about a 1000-acres of land. He sold his farm land in 1879 and moved to Canton, where he opened a commission house and became a freight agent on the Cumberland River. He was a member of the Grange and the Baptist church.

MADISON SIMS MAJOR (1820-1876). The last of Edgar's maternal great-uncles was "Mat" Major. He married Harriett Garrott and, with assistance from her father, they bought the 600-acre Blue Lantern farm on the Cadiz Road. He was stabbed to death by a farm tenant who was freed by the Christian County Grand Jury on the testimony that Major attacked first.

UNCLE JOHN. Edgar's mother's older brother, John Francis Major (1843-1872) was a farmer in the Beverly neighborhood who died less than two years after he married. This image was printed on a half-dollar size picture button, a popular method of wearing photographs over a century ago.

AUNT MOLLIE. In Edgar's boyhood, traveling even a short distance was a rare experience. His mother's oldest sister, Mary Bush Major Clardy (1840-1916) and her husband, James M. Clardy, initially lived on a farm across from Beverly Store. They later moved to "Woodlawn", the Clardy homeplace, located southeast of Bell Station, now the site of the Ft. Campbell airport. The Cayce family made occasional visits to a place they considered a great distance away, though not more than five miles.

REPUBLICAN UNCLE. The men in Edgar's family were Democrats. Edgar's maternal uncle, Thomas H. "Tom" Major (1850-1924), was an exception to the rule, both as a Republican and a member of the Baptist church at Locust Grove. This farmer, who married Mary W. Killen, served as a Constable and later as a Magistrate in the Longview district.

BEVERLY MERCHANT. George H. Major (1851-1928), Carrie's brother, was a farmer throughout his life, a merchant at Beverly, and postmaster in 1880-81. Members of his family have always maintained an interest in Edgar Cayce's psychic readings.

FARM WIFE. Anna Major Seargeant (1855-1926), Edgar's maternal aunt, her husband, Hugh Seargeant, and their daughters Mary and Susan lived on a farm on Huffman's Mill Road in south Christian County. She attended Bethel Female College in Hopkinsville and spent most of her life as a farm wife. Aunt "Annie" and her daughters later moved to Louisville, Kentucky where they maintained an extensive correspondence with Edgar Cayce and frequently called upon him for psychic readings.

RETRIEVED THE BODY. Word went out through the neighborhood on Wednesday afternoon, June 8, 1881, that Beverly neighborhood farmer, Tom Cayce, Edgar's paternal grandfather, had drowned in the farm pond in front of his home. The reputation of Lester "Les" Major (1859-1956), Edgar's mother's first cousin, a 21 year old fearless, aggressive man, prompted the family to seek him out to retrieve the body. Upon diving into the pond, Les located Tom's body entangled in barbed wire and brought it to the surface.

BOARDING COUSIN. J. Hugh Major (1883-1948) was a nephew of Edgar's mother, Carrie. He boarded with the family, then living on West Seventh Street, when he was a student at Major Ferrell's School in 1898-1899. He later attended dental school, but would spend his life as a machinist and working as a salesman for Planters Hardware Company and the Hopkinsville Implement Company.

LIFE GOES ON. These images of Edgar and Gertrude Cayce reveal the beauty, handsomeness, and hope for the future which they surely felt as the 20th-century dawned. The pictures were made circa 1900, some three years before their marriage. Ahead were the coming experiences of marriage, the birth of children, the death of a child, financial insecurity, court litigation, the negative reaction from their home community, but the continued love of a supportive family. A limited financial stability and negative public reaction to the "work" finally drove them from Hopkinsville to Anniston, Alabama in March, 1912. They later moved to Selma, Alabama; to Dayton, Ohio in November, 1923; and later settled at Virginia Beach, Virginia on September 16, 1925.

Chronology of the Formative Years
1877-1912

1877 – Edgar Cayce born near Beverly, Kentucky in Christian County

1883 – Began formal education in a schoolhouse behind Liberty Christian Church

1888 – Professed faith in Christ and united with Liberty Christian Church on October 13.

1889-1893 – Attended Beverly Academy, located between Beverly store and Liberty Church

1890 – Vision, followed by incident of spelling clairvoyance

1893 – Family moved to Hopkinsville in December, occupied home at 705 West Seventh, southeast corner Seventh and Young Streets.

1894-1898 – Edgar moved to Hopkinsville; First job at Richard's Dry Goods Store, then in Hopper's Bookstore; both located on Main Street; Relocated to Louisville, Kentucky.

1899 – Home for Christmas and decided to remain in Hopkinsville

1900 – Formed a business partnership with his father, L.B. Cayce, to sell Woodman of the World Insurance; severe illness in March; lost voice on April 18; went to Louisville on June 8 to take business course at Bryant & Stratton Business College; returned to Hopkinsville in the fall and began work in the photograph studio of W.R. Bowles at corner of Ninth and Virginia Streets.

1901 – "Hart-The Laugh Man," a hypnotist, put Edgar Cayce to sleep on the stage of Holland's Opera House and his voice returned – February 12, gave his first psychic medical reading March 31, recovered voice. Began readings for patients of Al C. Layne.

1902 – Frank H. Bassett, Sr. obtained for him a photographer's position in Bowling Green with Lucian D. Potter's Bookstore in May; roomed in the Boarding House of Mrs. Hollins with Dr. Hugh C. Beazley; gave readings in the Dietrich case.

1903 – Married Gertrude Evans, June 17.

1904 – Formed photographic studio partnership with Frank J. Potter, cousin of L.D. Potter in July.

1905 – Dalton case, resulting from fall sustained by George Dalton at the construction site of new L&N Railroad Freight Office, May 31.

1906 – Cayce Studio on College Street in Bowling Green conducted a $40,000 art exhibit of paintings, carbon prints, and water colors, opened in November; studio destroyed by fire on December 23.

1907 – Son Hugh Lynn Cayce born March 16; State Street Studio burned in September.

1909 – Moved family back to Hopkinsville, August. Worked that fall in Gadsden, Alabama; home for Christmas; conducted first psychic reading to be held in the Dalton Building, corner of Virginia and Seventh, in December.

1910 – Worked for Russell Bros., Photographers in Anniston, Alabama, January to July 4; then associated with H.P. Tressler, of Montgomery, Alabama, July to October. New York Times article appeared October 9; moved back to Hopkinsville and formed the Psychic Reading Corporation with Dr. Wesley Ketchum, Albert D. Noe, Sr., and L.B. Cayce; photographic studio opened on the second floor of Thompson Building, Main Street between Seventh and Eighth Streets; gave readings daily for the first time as "Psychic Diagnostician." Rented Mrs. Arnolds's cottage at 1910 South Main Street.

1911 – Roswell Field, brother of Eugene Field, with Hearst's Chicago Examiner, came to Hopkinsville in February to write a feature article of Edgar Cayce for the paper. In March, Edgar Cayce, L.B. Cayce and A.D. Noe, Sr. made a ten day trip to Chicago to give readings for the paper; son Milton Porter Cayce born on March 28 and died May 17; wife Gertrude suffered from tuberculosis, much improved within the first year.

1912 – Investigation by Dr. Hugo Munsterberg , of Harvard University; broke partnership with Dr. Ketchum and A.D. Noe, Sr., filed suit against them for $28,000 in Christian Circuit Court for breach of contract, (settled out of court in March, 1913); family moved to Anniston, Alabama in March; then to Selma to open photographic studio.